The Art of Exceptional Leadership

A Hands-On Guide for New Leaders

by

Robert Wohlfarth

Dedicated to my daughter Amanda who just started her leadership journey

Acknowledgments

I want to thank the myriad of people who helped me with this book. I reached out to hundreds of leaders to ask for their input and advice. Among those who provided substantial contributions and who were role models throughout my career are: Vince Corica, Jim Favero, Jay Gast, Dean Madison, and Dave Martin. Your input was invaluable and very much appreciated.

To my rock, my wife Darla, thank you for your support and tireless efforts. I love you.

I've learned that people will forget what you said, people will forget what you did, but people will never forget how you made them feel.

Maya Angelou

Contents

Introduction 11
Chapter 1-What is a Leader? 19
Chapter 2-Why Do You Want to Be a Leader? 22
Chapter 3-Vision vs Mission 24
Chapter 4-What is your core leadership philosophy? 27
Chapter 5-Key Traits of a Leader 30
Chapter 6-The Barnyard of Work Animals 35
Chapter 7-Moving from Peer to Leader 39
Chapter 8-Hiring-The Key to Building a Great Team 42
Chapter 9-Team Dynamics 48
Chapter 10-Leading Change 55
Chapter 11-Coaching 59
Chapter 12-Diversity/Equity/Inclusion 65
Chapter 13-Taking Disciplinary Action 70
Chapter 14-Handling Dysfunctional Teams 75
Chapter 15-Managing Virtual Teams 83
Chapter 16-Recognition 86
Chapter 17-Politics, Performance, and Perception 91
Summary 96

Introduction

> **"**
>
> After 30 years of leading teams, I still have so much to learn
>
> ROBERT WOHLFARTH

My leadership journey started rather inauspiciously. I was 22 years old, a recent college graduate and after being in a sales role for about a year and half and doing ok, I was promoted to lead a sales team in another city. I had no management experience, in fact, I never even thought about managing a team, but when they offered a city in Florida, my cold Pittsburgh bones said "Absolutely!" Little did I know the journey I would be embarking upon.

The team I was to take over was the most established and oldest team in the company. Most of the salespeople that worked there had more time in with the company than I had years on this earth. I was told by senior management that my job was to "shake things up" and get the office back on track. I vividly remember my first sales meeting with the team where I laid out some generic vision on where we wanted to go. I went through the historic performance numbers for each team member. I showed them that they had not achieved their revenue goals in months and that we needed to change things. I had not even met the entire team yet, but I was counting on my amazing charm, charisma, and, most importantly my title to get them to buy into the vision. Well, you might have already guessed how that meeting went. It was a complete dud. This was my introduction to leading teams, and I failed the test miserably. I was fired four months later.

The fact is that 60% of new managers fail within the first two years. Even knowing this fact now, it doesn't make me feel better about my failure. But it made me realize that I was definitely not ready to lead a team. I thought my title would be enough motivation, but in reality, titles mean little. Leadership requires a mind shift adjustment from "do what I say" to "how can I help you?". Serving your team is the most fundamental aspect of leadership.

Fortunately, I was able to get another leadership role and luckily, I found a mentor who helped me understand how to lead a team. This mentor showed me that without getting buy-in from the team, I was going nowhere fast. He provided me with my first true leadership lesson- "praise in public, criticize in private". I never forgot that lesson.

Recently, out of the blue, I received a note from a team member who worked with me that stunned me. When I hired her to lead our customer service team, she had no experience in leading a team and often took a heavy-handed approach to managing the team. I worked with her to help her understand the nuances of leading a team and coached her on how to handle the stress that comes with leading a team. But the note she sent thanked me for my leadership and stated that the lessons she learned during that time stuck with her and in times when a hard decision needed to be made or a tough situation arose, she would ask herself "WWBD- What would Bob do?" That note humbled me and it reinforced how important leaders can be in a person's life and how you can leave a legacy without realizing it.

The purpose of this book is to provide a guide for new leaders on how to effectively lead a team. I have tapped the wisdom of some of the best leadership minds I have had the great fortune to work with and unashamedly will "borrow" insights from other great authors on the subject. The key is to help you understand that leading people the right way can have a profound impact on their lives and also on yours.

I have studied leadership for over 30 years and have been fortunate to have worked with some amazing people. One of the best leaders I have had the great fortune to work with, Vincent Corica, Senior Vice President at MCI, uses the quote from Maya Angelou, "I've learned that people will forget what you said, people will forget what you did, but people will never forget how you made them feel" as his guiding principle. Vince, a highly decorated Vietnam War veteran, led a very large team at MCI, but when you spoke with him, you felt like you were the most important person in the world. He lived that quote and as a result of this type of leadership, people were willing to walk through walls for Vince. His team outperformed every team in the company and did so on a consistent basis. It is important it is to live your values as a leader. Vince did that every day.

Leading a team of any size can be exhilarating, frustrating, but so rewarding. It is a position of trust to be taken seriously. In this book, I will share some wisdom I have gathered through the years and provide some foundation for creating a legacy-based leadership model for yourself.

Sun Tzu, the author of The Art of War, states this take on leadership "Leadership is a matter of intelligence, trustworthiness, humaneness, courage and sternness. When one has all 5 virtues together, then one can be a leader". While I agree with most of this, I believe the foundation of true leadership is a unique blend of humility and confidence. As a leader, your role is to effect performance through your team members. While that is the primary purpose, you also have a secondary purpose as a leader. Your goal as a leader is to not only positively impact the performance of your team, but, ultimately, your role is to make your team members better people.

Great leaders can change your life. You may have had a teacher or coach that positively impacted you long after the class or sport ended. Or you may have had a boss that believed in you when no one else did.

Growing up, I boxed at a local neighborhood gym that was coached by a legendary leader named Chuck Senft. Chuck, another decorated Army Veteran, worked for the Parks Department for the city of Pittsburgh. He was a stocky man and the first thing you noticed about Chuck was his head of coal black hair that he was able to somehow, against all the laws of physics, grease into a cresting wave that just didn't move.

He took over a very run-down, drug-riddled, local park and began working with youths, most of who were troubled. There were several times he went home tired, bruised, and sore as he often had to physically disarm kids in the park. One time he had to rescue a 10-year-old child who was surrounded by a group of 5 older kids intent on beating him up. That 10-year-old was me. Being on the smaller size for my age, he convinced me to join his growing boxing club to help me defend myself. I took him up on it and it changed my life. Not so much for the boxing skills, as I was never a great boxer, but it was the discipline he instilled in my life. At that time where I grew up, there were basically two choices-play sports or do drugs. Again, being a smaller than average kid, I couldn't play the traditional sports of football or basketball and I was terrible at baseball. So that left boxing where you are matched according to weight.

Chuck provided an atmosphere of inclusion where every member of "Charlie's Angels", the name of the boxing club, felt safe and a part of the team. As you know, boxing is an individual sport, but Chuck created a tight-knit team. We all were members of the team and we all rooted for each other, cried with each other after tough losses and became brothers in a rather violent sport. There were three elements to Chuck's success. He treated everyone the same-he was equally tough on everyone, and he had no favorites, and everyone was a member of the team regardless of their experience or standing. If one person decided to slack off during one of the grueling exercises, he put us through, we all paid the price. There were no cliques despite the fact that we had a wide array of talent from pure beginners to state, regional and national champion boxers. Everyone was welcome to join, and we all looked out for each other, in the gym and on the street. Second, he instilled discipline into our lives. He pushed us physically past what any of us thought were possible. He relentlessly drilled us on the fundamentals. And thankfully so, as three 3-minute rounds don't sound like much, but believe me it is, and in those moments when you thought you had no more to give, you found a way and relied on your training. And three, he genuinely cared about each and every one of us. Most nights there were over 100 kids in that gym training to become one of "Charlie's Angels". If you skipped a training session, you can be sure that Chuck called your house looking for you, I can honestly say that without Chuck and his leadership, my life would have gone in a completely different direction.

He didn't demand respect so much as he commanded our respect. He understood that even though we were just poor kids from the inner city, we were worthy of respect and worthy of his time. He truly cared about each and every kid and it didn't matter if you were a Golden Gloves champ or not. He made being one of Charlie's Angel cool and respectable. And at the year-end banquet, we made darn sure we had sold enough candy or popcorn to earn that coveted "Charlie's Angels" jacket which we would wear proudly.

As leaders, we don't just generate results from a team. We often change people's lives in ways we cannot fathom. Chuck devoted his entire life to his role and whether he knew it or not, he positively influenced hundreds, if not thousands, of lives. His legacy lives on in several of his boxers who continued his tradition. The impact he had was immeasurable.

I didn't get a chance to truly thank him for all he did and the lessons he taught me, but I will never forget him.

Rest in peace Coach.

> Exceptional leaders don't make their teams better workers, they make their teams better humans

ROBERT WOHLFARTH

Leading a team is an amazing experience but one that comes with very serious responsibilities. As the leader, please understand you own the overall performance of the entire team. If they fail, you fail. If they succeed, you succeed. But true leaders never take the credit for the work their team has done. They deflect the credit to the team. This is the humility part of leadership. We have all seen or worked for leaders (most likely managers), who take complete credit for their team's success, and they will throw their team under the proverbial bus when things do not go as planned.

The problem is not that the person managing the team is a bad person, often, they are not. It is simply a matter of how they perceive their role and how they were trained. Often, I see organizations promote people into leadership roles with little to no experience on how to actually lead people. They may be experts at getting the job done and understand the position very well, but they are not trained on the nuances of leading a team. It is often "trial by fire" and this is unfair to the leader and definitely unfair to the team.

Simply put, exceptional leaders are servants, and the best ones, lead from the heart.

This book was written to assist you in the journey and provide guidance on how to lead teams. This is not your typical leadership book that is long on philosophy and short of real-world advice. It is a hands-on guide for the new leader.

Chapter 1 - What is a Leader?

> Leaders say "we should"
> Managers say "you should"
>
> ROBERT WOHLFARTH

How does a leader differ from a manager? The best definition I have ever heard on this subject is that a leader leads people while a manager manages processes.

There are other key differences as well. Leaders tend to pull people forward while managers tend to push. It is also described as leading from in front, instead of from behind. It is an example of "do what I say, not what I do".

Most of us have worked with people who inspired us, sometimes kicked our butts, but they motivated us to become better every single day. We also probably worked with people who micro-managed us and annoyed us to the point where we left or wanted to leave.

Are these two philosophies mutually exclusive in terms of getting the job done? No, often you will see companies with great managers hitting all the key numbers, but their teams often perform more out of fear than anything else. Often, I find the leaders in organizations are not the ones with the title, but someone underneath them who garners the real power. This is the power of influence.

As the leader of a team, your primary role is to generate results from your team. This can be done in a number of ways. A true leader often leads from the heart. Managers often lead only with the head. True leaders provide a vision for their teams. Managers provide objectives. This doesn't mean leaders don't set objectives, they do, but they set them in concert with achieving their overall vision. They provide their team with a higher purpose.

Early in my career, I entered the nascent long-distance telecommunications field with MCI. They are now, ironically, part of Verizon, which was formerly Bell Atlantic, and one of our fiercest competitors. This was a field that was dominated by big, bad AT&T and her sister Bell operating companies. For over a decade, we battled at every turn. Looking back, I wonder how we did it. We asked customers to dial 23 extra digits just to make a long-distance call. We had equipment ripped off the walls and thrown into the garbage. We encountered a fight at every corner. But the thing that kept us going was the vision and the mission of freeing our customers from paying too much for calls. This vision drove all of the behavior in the company, and it permeated the entire organization. It helped us overcome the day-to-day challenges we encountered. We relished the challenge of battling the giant, AT&T.

Creating your own vision and mission statements are critical to your success as a leader. They provide your team with the framework on how to perform their role. As a leader you probably do not want to get involved in every single decision your team faces every day. Vision and mission statements allow your team to make decisions based on this framework. For instance, as an example, one of the components of your vision is to be customer-centric and to take care of the customer at all times, and a disgruntled customer calls in and registers a complaint about your product requesting a refund or replacement, then your team should feel comfortable handling that request without much in the way of approval. But let's say they went over and above in their role and exceeded their limit in an effort to appease the customer. While some managers will discipline the person, the true leader understands the context in which they made this decision was in accordance with their vision and mission.

Chapter 2-Why Do You Want to Be a Leader?

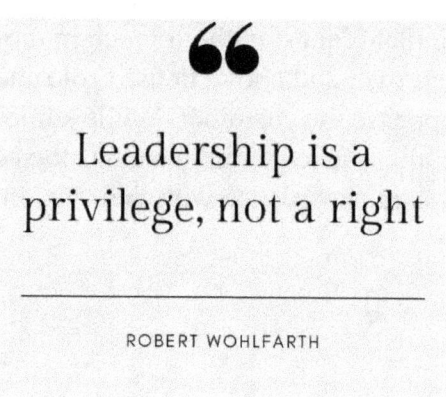

> Leadership is a privilege, not a right
>
> ROBERT WOHLFARTH

Leading a team is much tougher than it might appear. Even when everything is going well, it is hard. When things are not going well, it is exceedingly difficult. Leading a team is much more than telling people what to do. It is about coaching and serving. It is about having to have very difficult, often life changing conversations with people, especially if you have to terminate their employment.

If you wish to lead a team because you love the power that comes with it, then it is probably not for you. If, on the other hand, you wish to lead a team to help others succeed, then you are on the right track.

People often say that leadership is a natural talent. I am not so sure about that. I believe that some of the basics, like empathy and the desire to help people are inherent, but most leadership skills can be learned.

The key thing to keep in mind is that as a leader you work for your team, not the other way around. If you keep this mantra close to your heart, you will do well.

Chapter 3-Vision vs Mission

> True leaders provide a vision and a mission.
>
> Managers provide objectives.
>
> ROBERT WOHLFARTH

As we discussed earlier, true leaders excel at creating a vision and a mission for their teams. But there is often confusion about these two words. Sometimes they are used interchangeably, and this is not correct.

A vision is what we want to be. What is the long-term goal of the company or department? Think of it more as a long-term goal achieved over years.

A mission statement is how do we get there. What steps do we need to take to achieve our vision?

To give you an example: Assume you work in a hospice facility and were recently tapped to lead a team of caregivers tasked with taking care of the facilities residents during the remainder of their lives. What is your vision? Is it to provide adequate care or is it to provide an extraordinary level of care and ensure the residents are exceptionally well cared for in their remaining days?

So, your vision statement may be: To provide an exceptional level of care for our patients.

But how do you do that? That is your mission statement. The mission statement provides guidance to the team for everyday tasks.

Your mission statement might be:

      -Compassion-deliver care with deeply embedded compassion

      -Comfort-Ensure patients are kept comfortable at all times

      -Communication-Keep family members aware of the patient's condition

While this is just an example in what may be one of the most challenging of fields, you can perform this exercise with your own organization by asking a few questions:

Vision

-What is our overarching goal?

-What do we want to have accomplished in 10 years?

-What do we want to world to know us for?

Mission

-What steps do we need to take to get there?

-What are the absolutes in terms of how we act?

-What key components define our behavior?

Establishing your vision and mission statements will provide a roadmap of sorts for you to handle your team and set the tone for what is acceptable and what is unacceptable behaviors.

Chapter 4 - What is your core leadership philosophy?

> **Exceptional leaders have a set of core operating principles and never waver from them**
>
> ROBERT WOHLFARTH

The best leaders often have a code they live by. These are a key set of core operating principles that define them and, more importantly, define their actions. These are non-negotiable principles of how they conduct themselves and how they expect their teams to act.

Often these philosophies are rather simple. They are the rules of engagement that permeate the entire organization. They set the tone for everyone and provide team members with guidance on how to handle situations and generally run-in conjunction with their vision and mission statements.

Konosuke Matsushita, the founder of Panasonic in Japan, is known in that country as the "god of management" for his writings and speeches on leadership and management. He wrote, "If you are a leader, you must have an ideology of leadership. If you lack an ideology and attempt to decide everything on a case-by-case basis, you will never be capable of strong leadership."

One of the best leaders I have ever worked with, Jay Gast, has a very strong and succinct set of core operating principle-5 C's-Clarity, Consistency, Commitment, Collaboration and Customer. These principles have served him well throughout his career and it made it easier to understand his perspective as you knew where he stood on issues. He relied on his core operating philosophy.

My core operating philosophy is FED:

Focus-focus relentlessly on the customer.

Execution-execute at the highest level possible.

Discipline-be disciplined in your daily habits and ask your team to do the same.

Your core operating philosophy takes the guesswork away from your team and provides them with guidance on what is expected in terms of behavior. I have found that most disciplinary actions within companies come as a result of people not knowing how to properly do their role and as a result, causing mistakes to be made. I operate from the principle that most people want to do a good job. For the most part, this has worked well. At times, yes, I have been burned when someone took advantage of my trust, but overall, this was rare.

Create your own Core Operating Philosophy by asking the questions:

-What behaviors do I value? Is it honesty, trustworthiness, dedication, attention to detail?

-What behaviors are completely unacceptable? Perhaps lying, cheating, stealing?

Figure out what your core philosophy is, and you will have the basis of your leadership style. Use this as the foundation of your leadership journey. And it is a journey. You will never know all the answers and when you think you have seen it all, you will find something that challenges you. That is the nature of leading people. They are unpredictable and sometimes maddening, but it is an extremely rewarding journey.

Chapter 5-Key Traits of a Leader

> Humility is the foundation of a good leader
>
> ROBERT WOHLFARTH

There are a few key components to leadership that are critical to your success.

They are humble-exceptional leaders are humble. They understand that they need to be confident in their approach, but they also know they may not have all of the answers. They deflect praise to their team and accept responsibility when things go awry.

They are authentic-true leaders are authentic in their approach. They are comfortable in their own skin and do not play games with people's minds. As Popeye the cartoon character stated, "I yam what I yam and that's all that I yam". True leaders live that phrase every day.

They communicate up and down the organization-great leaders are excellent communicators and can do so on multiple levels. They understand verbal and non-verbal communication. They are explicit and clear in their communication. If they believe that there may not be a proper level of understanding, they will repeat or rephrase, as necessary.

They are consistent-truly great leaders are consistent in their approach. Have you ever had a boss that was moody and unpredictable? You often waited for the "right time" to tell them bad news, right? Good leaders present the same "face" every day. It is important that your team members know what to expect every day.

They are intelligent-There are two types of intelligence-IQ and EQ. While, traditional intelligence is important, I have found truly exceptional leaders most often have a great EQ or emotional quotient and are emotionally intelligent.

Emotional intelligence is often the defining factor in the success of failure of a leader.

Emotional intelligence (EI), emotional leadership (EL), emotional quotient (EQ) and emotional intelligence quotient (EIQ), is the capability of individuals to recognize their own emotions and those of others, discern between different feelings and label them appropriately. Effective leaders use emotional information to guide thinking and behavior and manage and/or adjust emotions to adapt to environments or achieve one's goal(s). Although the term first appeared in 1964, it gained popularity in the 1995 book Emotional Intelligence, written by the science journalist Daniel Goleman.[4]

The key components to EI are:

Self-awareness-this is the ability to truly understand yourself, your emotions, and your effect on the world around you.

Self-regulation-this is your ability to control your own emotions. I always laugh when I see the manager of a baseball team screaming at the umpires and think, wow, that wouldn't work in the real world.

Motivation-this is referring to intrinsic motivation or that motivation that comes from within you. Leading a team can offer extremely high levels of euphoria, but it can also provide you with very low points as well. It is these radical changes, often within the same day which can deplete your motivation. Remember, your team is looking to you for guidance and they will take cues, often non-verbal cues, on how to act in certain situations.

Empathy-Empathy is a core component of an emotionally intelligent leader. The ability to put yourself in other's shoes and see things from their perspective is critical to your success as a leader.

Social skills-Another key attribute of an emotionally intelligent leader is their ability to be at ease in virtually any social situation. They are comfortable in their own skin and make others around them feel comfortable. Some of this comes from maintaining a non-judgmental attitude. They actively listen to understand, not just to respond.

They have integrity-Integrity is a vital element of leadership. There will be numerous times when your integrity will be tested in a leadership role. Your team members or senior leadership may put you in a tenuous position. Never compromise your integrity.

They are trustworthy- Following on the previous trait, it is important that your team members know they can trust you. I had a manager once that worked for me who was entrusted with a rather delicate secret that one of his team members shared with him. This manager broke the trust when he shared this with certain team members who then shared it with others. Soon, the entire office knew much to the dismay of the person who shared the secret. He lost the trust of his team and it cost him. Your team may share very personal details with you, and it is crucial that you maintain that level of trust.

They are confident but not egotistical-Leaders exude a level of confidence that is reassuring, but they are not egotistical. While this sounds easy, it is sometimes hard not to let your ego drive decisions. Confident leaders have faith in their abilities and believe in themselves. Ego is something else entirely. It is driven out of self-interest and often is exhibited as a defensive posture. Ego looks for accolades and validation over everything else. It is often recognized through self-aggrandizement. Confident leaders let their teams take the credit for their work and work hard to recognize their team members for their contributions.

They are disciplined- Leaders are disciplined in their daily habits. They are often the first ones in the office and are consistent in how they approach their day.

They are selfless- Leaders understand that their success is reliant on the success of their team members, and they are more concerned with the needs of their teams. This might mean taking a shift when a team member has a sick child with no reprisal. They understand that their team members have families and are always willing to pitch in and help.

They are focused- Leaders tend to stay focused on the most important items. It is easy to get lost in minutia and leaders tend to be able to reorder their priorities and stay focused on the goals they set for their team.

They are adept at handling setbacks- Leaders know that there will be setbacks and they don't get upset when they occur. They take them in stride and focus more on how we can avoid them in the future rather than assigning blame.

They embrace failure- While no one wants to fail, leaders take a long-term view and understand that sometimes people fail, and they use these failures as motivation and seek to understand the root causes and work with their team to eliminate those.

They take risks- Leaders understand that taking risks is essential to moving the organization forward. They are also adept at minimizing the downside of these risks, but they understand that failure may be the result and are okay with this outcome.

They are humane- Leaders know that while they have goals and objectives, they are first and foremost, dealing with human beings who have feelings, families, personal issues, and issues that may impact their work. Leaders are benevolent and compassionate and care deeply for those entrusted in their care.

While there are many traits that define a leader, maybe the biggest one is that they care deeply about their team. They are looking for subtle signs that maybe something isn't right before it becomes a bigger problem.

Chapter 6-The Barnyard of Work Animals

As you progress through your career, you come across multiple personalities in the workplace. Some are fantastic and wonderful to work with, and others, not so much. There are a lot of personality profiling services like Myers-Briggs, DISC, and many others, and they are generally very accurate, but this is a light-hearted way of looking at office personalities.

A few to be aware of are:

The Rooster-this is a loud, brash, and narcissistic person. They strut around and are annoying to virtually everyone they meet. They are often great performers, but the key issue here is that they just don't see themselves the way others do. They tend to lack empathy, emotional intelligence, and are hard to train and harder to coach. You can tell a Rooster by how they start a conversation-it usually starts bombastically with "Well, I….". This is a difficult personality to lead, but with patience, it can be done.

The Hen-mother hen is often the one who keeps the team together. They plan the team outings; they remember birthdays and are essential to the overall well-being of the team. Recognizing their value with thoughtful praise and appreciation will keep them happy.

The Goat-Often highly intelligent, these people are often the ones pushing the boundaries and recommending brash, new ideas. They are also essential, but they have to be carefully managed as they can be a bit ornery and will often do things on their own. They tend to challenge status quo and can be headstrong. It is best to give them some leeway and listen to their ideas but be sure to set firm boundaries with them.

The Donkey-You will recognize this person by the perpetually sour look on their faces. They don't like to try new things and tend to want to cling to the old ways. They are hard to train, and difficult to manage, but because of their tenure, they often exert a lot of influence over the group. It is best to work with them one on one to convince them to give new ideas a try. Once you have them on board, they make life a little easier for you.

The Sheep- This person generally goes along with the crowd. They tend not to make waves and usually are good employees. They are often risk averse and usually just want to put in their time and go home. While they are usually good employees, they will most likely not contribute a lot to the team beyond their job description.

The Bull-this person tends to try to overpower everyone and doesn't take other people's ideas and feelings into consideration. This usually includes the leader. They will often ignore the leader's wishes and just do what they want. This person is deadly to building a team culture, if left unchecked. But if you can get their buy-in, it will help your cause. It is often best to work with them behind the scenes and enlist their support as they will often use public forums to voice their opinions.

The Fox-This sly rascal will often undermine your authority and often be the source of gossip and innuendo. They are smart in how they go about this and will create havoc on your team. They work behind the scenes rather than direct like the bull. You might find that they are often the "teacher's pet" but use the information they obtain for nefarious purposes.

The best course of action with this person is to take them aside, let them know that you know what they are doing and let them know that if they have differing opinions on how things should be done, to please let you know. But make it clear that you cannot tolerate backstabbing.

The Stallion-this thoroughbred is a leader's dream. They are strong employees who take coaching well. They tend to outperform their colleagues, but they are not egotistical about it. They take a team first approach and will support the leader and their initiatives. This person generally thrives on recognition and will respond well to it. But be wary that other team members may be tired of hearing how good this person is.

The Pig-this person is often a great employee, and they perform well, but they are physically untidy. You can identify them by the hundreds of post-It notes on their walls. But the interesting thing is that they know where everything is, and this is just their system. It is often best to leave them be as trying to disrupt their system will cause them stress.

The Duck- they tend to bring a lot of personal issues into the workplace. They are the ones who are always on the phone with their ducklings, I mean, kids or their spouse/partner, and are usually dealing with some kind of issue. They tend to be easily distracted and will often require a very structured approach and firm boundaries at work. They tend to be high maintenance and require quite a bit of coaching and reiteration. Just be careful not to allow their personal issues to spill over into the workplace and affect the team.

The Owl-this is the person who has been there a very long time. They have deep institutional knowledge and know the short-cuts and more importantly, the people who can get things done. They are well respected and can be a tremendous asset to you in your quest to lead the team. But don't expect them to be on board in the beginning as they may have been through a large number of managers, and they are a bit jaded. But enlisting their support will go a long way as they have a lot of influence, and the team often looks to them for guidance.

Chapter 7-Moving from Peer to Leader

> Moving from peer to leader is one of the toughest roles
>
> ROBERT WOHLFARTH

Congratulations, you just got a promotion to team leader!

Hold on though, there's going to be a few things you need to know.

First, your old teammates are no longer teammates. They are now your responsibility. It is up to you whether they succeed or fail. Leading a team is an honor and a tremendous responsibility. While you were working together, it was ok to gossip (actually it's never good to gossip!), it was OK to talk negatively about that new pricing model everyone hates (that wasn't good either) or it was OK to go out and have a few beers and just let loose (I hope there were no pictures!). Now that you are carrying the company flag, none of these kinds of behaviors are OK. Your team will be looking to you to LEAD them.

You will be tested in your new role, of that there will be no doubt. The person that is a good friend but is habitually late to the team meetings will look for you to be OK with it. Don't validate the behavior. Pull him/her aside and let them know, this is not going to work and that their behavior needs to change. You will be tested at every turn, so be aware of it and face it head on and directly. In other words, take charge.

Second, not everyone is going to be rooting for you. The chances are, someone else from your team tried out for the position and didn't get it. While not everyone is vindictive, keep your eyes and ears open for behavior that may be undermining your team. These may be behaviors as flippant as openly questioning one of your initiatives or as subtle as negative body language. I have found that directly approaching the person early on and discussing the situation and enlisting their support goes a long way. You may ask them to help you and in return, you will help position them for the next leadership role.

Third, leading people is completely different than only being responsible for you and your sales numbers or your project. Sometimes it is like herding chickens. The best advice I can give you is to communicate clearly and consistently what your expectations are and 'inspect what you expect". Create a daily, weekly, monthly cadence so your new team knows exactly what is expected of them and when. Create a sense of accountability and discipline but understand that these are people with emotions and family issues and problems outside the workplace that may be affecting their behavior. Don't be heavy handed and stay engaged with your team so you can spot the subtle changes that often portend major workplace behavioral issues.

Truly, the hardest part of leading a team is having to let someone go. Unless it is an egregious offense, I tend to err on the side of the employee whenever possible. I innately believe that most people are good and that they want to do a good job, but sometimes they don't know how to do it correctly or they are having personal issues. That is up to you to ensure they have every tool and have been given every chance to succeed. If it is a personal issue, please make sure you help them wherever possible. Most companies have Employee Assistance Programs to help them sort out their issues. Only after exhausting all avenues of assistance, should you terminate their employment. But on the flip side, if you make a hiring mistake and you know there is no chance for this employee due to attitude, lack of desire or they just are not a good fit, move fast to get them off the team. One negative person can ruin an entire team. Tolerating a poor performer sends a message to everyone and this will impact your top performers the most.

Fourth, enjoy the ride. Leading a team is such a rewarding experience. There will be times of exhilaration and times of frustration, but always remember to check your ego at the door and keep the best interests of your team first and you will succeed.

Good luck and congratulations on your promotion!

Chapter 8-Hiring-The Key to Building a Great Team

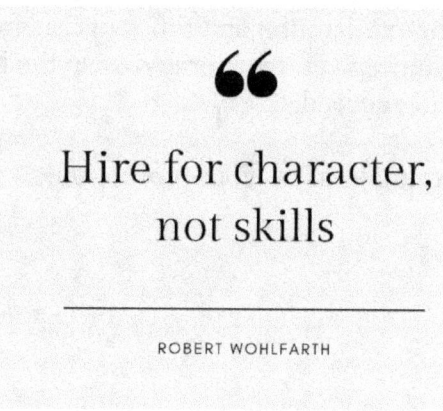

Jim Collins, in his book *Good to Great*, has as one of his first rules, to get the right people in the right seats on the bus. This quote stuck with me. A great leader can do a lot of things to positively impact a company, but if you have the wrong people on board, there is nothing that you can do as a leader to change your outcome. It is critical to have people in the right role, being happy and productive.

Your initial evaluation should be "Do I have the right team in place?" If not, ask "what are they missing-is it skill or is it will?" If your team is missing critical skills, train them. It is always much better, and much less expensive to train an existing employee than to go hire a new one. According to studies, the average cost of hiring a new employee is about one year's worth of salary, when you consider recruitment, lost production, and time.

If it is a "will" issue, then this will require a serious conversation between you and the employee. Sit the employee down and have a discussion with them to determine what the issues might be. Are they not happy with their role? Are they having issues at home? Are there other factors that might be impacting their work? Can they change their attitude? If not, it might be best to remove the person to another role or unfortunately terminate their employment.

Hiring great team members is an art. I often see leaders who hire people who are just like them. They think the same. They act the same. Sometimes they even dress the same. Most of the time these teams fail to achieve their goals due to the lack of diversity. While there is no sure-fire formula for hiring great team members, there are a few things you can do to help.

One of the best leaders I have ever worked for, Dave Martin, had a succinct philosophy he termed *GAS*. He summed it up to me in 6 words "Hire People Who Give a Shit". In other words, hire people who are passionate about what they do.

I believe that hiring excellent team members comes down to four rules:

1. **Looking beyond the resume**-with the proliferation of professional resume services, it is easy to have a fantastic resume. Studies have shown that 85% of people have lied on their resume! Whether these are omissions or outright lies, the result is the same-the

person is being untruthful. I would rather have someone on my team that was honest about their previous role, even if it did result in a termination, than someone who lied about it.

Some things to look for when you are evaluating a resume are:

- Length of stay in each role. If the person changed jobs every 2 years, that is a pretty good indication that they wore out their welcome as it often takes 2 years to move a person through the termination process

- Progression-did they get promoted at previous roles? If so, that's a pretty good sign that they excelenled in their role

- Grammatical/Spelling errors-this indicates a lack of attention to detail, and you can probably expect this to be the case in your department as well.

- Look for their accomplishments-did they improve their department in some way? Just keep in mind that this is the area where most people are likely to lie. As a sales leader, I never found anyone who wasn't in the "top 10% "of their sales team. I often ask for written proof of accomplishments or reference letters from previous supervisors. I also compare their resume to their LinkedIn profile to see if there is a difference.

2. **Asking the right questions**-Interviewees are well schooled now on answering the standard questions interviewers ask such as "Tell

me why you feel like you are a fit for this role?" or "What are your strengths or weaknesses?"

Asking behavioral oriented questions such as listed below tend to provide more insight into their thought process and force them to provide more detail on how they handled certain situations. Some of the most effective questions are:

- *Tell me about a time you disagreed with your boss? How did you handle that?*

- *Give me an example of a time you faced a conflict while working on a team. How did you handle that?*

- *Describe a time when you struggled in your position. How did you eventually overcome that?*

- *We all make mistakes we wish we could take back. Tell me about a time you wish you had handled a situation differently at work?*

- *Give me an example of a time when you did not meet a client's expectation. What happened, and how did you attempt to rectify the situation?*

- *Describe a time when you had to interact with a difficult client. What was the situation, and how did you handle it?*

- *When you are working with a firm deadline, how do you go about prioritizing your tasks?*

These types of questions will force the applicant to provide real world examples and give you a better idea of how they may perform in your organization. Just change the questions to fit your particular need.

Another question I like to ask is "why". I use this to clarify their thoughts and actions. Questions such as "why did you choose to do it that way?" or "why do you think there was a conflict with your team members?". This secondary questioning technique often provides additional details into an interviewee's thoughts and will provide some insight as to whether they are truthful or not.

Keep in mind that some people, especially those that have had numerous jobs are often very good at interviews. They know the right thing to say and have studied the answers to standard questions. Your job is to peel back the layers and get to the true person and behavioral questions tend to be the best way to do that.

3. **Check them out**-Google them and look at their social media feeds-I once wanted to hire a fellow for a sales role who was evidently a superstar and absolutely aced the interview. By chance, I took a peek at his social media feeds and found highly inflammatory comments along with racist statements and posts. I immediately terminated the process. Another person I was contemplating hiring had a side business selling hard to find parts for Porsche's and BMW's which was ok. But what I found out through a simple Google search was that he ripped off hundreds of people and took their money but never sent the parts. He had thousands of people looking for him. I didn't need that kind of drama in the office and if he had no issue ripping off that many people, he didn't belong on my team.

Just be careful to ensure that you actually have the right person when searching and if you have questions, reach out to your HR or Legal team. They often have access to products that can pull every comment they have ever made on social media. I highly recommend also doing a thorough background check on potential new hires as well.

4. **Get 360-degree feedback**-before I hire anyone, I always have them sit in on a team interview or an interview with another leader in the company. Often it is both. I preface this to them by telling them this is their chance to ask real world questions about the daily duties and the role. It also gives your team a chance to meet with them and see if they click. It is amazing to see what often comes out of these team interviews. I have had people admit to my team members that they really don't have the experience and I actually had one guy blatantly pass gas in the team interview and laugh about it. His comment was "I thought I was among friends!" Needless to say, we did not hire this fellow. Remember that you should take your time when hiring new team members. It is very expensive to hire and then have to terminate someone. You lose the money, but you also lose the time and production. It is always better to hire slow and if they are not a fit, fire fast.

Chapter 9-Team Dynamics

> Exceptional leaders put their team's needs ahead of their own
>
> ROBERT WOHLFARTH

Once you have your team on board, you enter a new phase where team dynamics begin to shape the unit's behavior. Team dynamics are fascinating to watch and study.

Have you ever worked in a place where things just clicked? Everyone was tight and everyone knew their roles, but they were not shy to suggest improvements. Communication was easy, open, and consistent.

On the flip side, you may have worked in a place where co-workers constantly sniped at each other or undermined each other. This is group dynamics in play.

As a leader, you have a lot of influence on the dynamics of your team. You set the tone for how the team interacts and behaves. Teams will take their cues on how to act from you. If you gossip, they will too. If you are moody, they will be as well. If you tolerate poor behavior, they will deliver. One of the hardest parts of being a leader is to continually be a model of consistency. We may not feel good, or we may have had a disagreement with a partner that left us in a bad mood, but we still have to show up and provide leadership to the team.

Understand that your leadership will be tested, especially in the beginning. Like small children, team members may see where the boundaries lie. They may try to get you to engage in favoritism and try influence peddling. These first few days, weeks and months will set the tone for your entire leadership experience with this team. The decisions you make now will form the basis of the team and it is critical to start off correctly.

So how do you build a strong team? There are a number of steps you can take to move the team toward becoming a strong, cohesive unit.

- **Create a shared vision.** The difference between a team and a group is that a team has a shared goal and purpose. This is the glue that binds the team together and it is crucial that you have teamwide commitment to the vision. They need to *want* to achieve this vision together.
- **Trust**-Every great team has an innate level of trust among the team members. Steven Covey, the author who penned the famous book *7 Habits of Highly Effective People* writes about the impact trust has in a business unit in his book, *The Speed of Trust* that *"(Strategy x Execution) x Trust = Results"*. An organization that is built upon the foundation of trust is an organization that will be agile, fast, and it will be able to quickly respond to competitive pressures. Organizational trust is based on integrity. That is everyone has to trust that each person in the organization will do their part, and everyone has trust in everyone else. According to Mr. Covey, high trust organizations outperform low trust organizations by 3X. That isn't to say that there will not be mistakes made, there will. It's that high trust organizations tend to

focus on getting continually better and treat mistakes as learning opportunities. Low trust organizations tend to push minor decisions up to the highest levels. I once did some consulting work with an organization where every single expenditure had to be approved by a Vice President. I asked why they did this, and their answer was to control costs. I asked the CEO if he trusted his people and he said, "yes, I do". I told him that having to have a VP sign off on $100 of basic office supplies indicated otherwise. Trust is the foundation of every great company. But this trust has to go both ways. In order to gain trust, you have to give trust.

- **Open communication**- As in any relationship, open and honest communication is integral to keeping the relationship whole. Sometimes this communication may be emotional, or it may take the form of snippy emails, or it may be passive/aggressive. As the leader, you will need to share with your team how to communicate effectively. You may have to work with them continually to ensure that the communication is direct, but not personal. As we know, different people may take the same sentence completely differently, depending on their perspective.
- **Clarity**-One of the most important things that you as a leader must do is to provide clarity to your team. What is expected? How should they handle their role? What are their objectives? This is part of the vision and mission of the team, and it should be consistently discussed. There is no place for obfuscation in the workplace.
- **Consistency**-Leaders need to be consistent in their dealings with their teams. While you may manage different people in different ways, it is important to be consistent in how you approach the role and how you deal with your team.

I remember in one of my early leadership roles that I had a team member who always showed up late for everything. I inherited this team from another manager and was trying to evaluate the team. This person was late to team meetings, they were late to client calls, they were late every morning. I had a discussion with this person and shared with her that I expected everyone to be on time for work and she said that the previous manager never minded because she was the "glue that held the team together". Granted she was very good at her job, but I could not allow her to continue with this path regardless. I went through a progressive disciplinary scenario with her (verbal warning, written warning, final written warning) and unfortunately had to terminate her employment due to this problem. After I informed the team, they actually applauded. It was obvious they didn't appreciate her actions either.

- **Willingness to tolerate mistakes**-We all know that mistakes can and will happen in every company. As a leader, it is our job to try to minimize them where possible. But when they do happen, work to find out the root cause and see how you can eliminate those errors moving forward. Shaming the person who caused them does not solve the problem. Remember the adage- *"Praise in public, criticize in private"*. While there should be a tolerance for honest mistakes, there should be little tolerance for sloppy work, continued mistakes of the same kind or overall careless work. Tolerating complacency and carelessness will affect the whole team.
- **Diversity and Inclusion**-Diversity and inclusion are incredibly important for every team. As humans, we work from our own basis of understanding. It is a matter of where we were born, how we were raised and our internal belief systems. We have unconscious bias in how we see the world. It is not wrong; it just is what it is. Having a diverse and inclusive team means that everyone feels safe to express their beliefs. Sometimes leaders tend to build "look-a-like" teams where everyone acts and sometimes even looks like the leader. They prescribe to the same beliefs, and they tend to think the same way. This type of team is generally not successful over the long term. Embrace diversity for all of the wonderfulness it can bring to your team. Make sure every member of the team feels included in the team's mission.

- **Interdependence and a Sense of Belonging-**There is nothing more satisfying than belonging to a strong, healthy team. Great teams are powerful, and they are collectively way more than the sum of the parts. But to get here, it's important to ensure that each member of the team understand and does their part within the framework of the team. Have you ever wondered why certain teams excel over a long period? This interdependence and belief in a higher purpose is why. I would rather have a team of average performers who believe in what we are doing than an entire team of superstars who look out only for themselves. Great teams care for each other, they support each other, and they help each other.
- **Consensus Decision Making-**While yes, you are the leader, it is important to understand that involving the team in decisions will help to solidify and strengthen the team. Feeling a part of the decision process is what helps teams grow and helps them understand each other's perspective. Ultimately, the decisions are yours, but garnering input will provide better data with which to decide.
- **Participative Leadership-**Providing each team member with a leadership role also will strengthen the team. If someone is responsible for a subsegment of a product, they should "own it" and have some say in its design and production. Think of an automobile manufacturer where there are thousands of interdependent parts that have to work together. Each team or person has to own their particular segment and they should be the ones who make the decisions on that part.

Team dynamics is a beautiful thing to watch, and it is probably the most satisfying aspect of being a leader to see a team come together to achieve what was thought to be impossible. But keep in mind that a team is a very fragile thing. It can break quite easily with one misstep.

Bruce Tuckman, a word renowned expert on team dynamics, uses the terms Forming, Storming, Norming, Performing, and Mourning, to illustrate the stages which groups go through.

- **Forming**-is the initial stage and is where team members get acquainted with each other. They are usually polite as they get to know each other.
- **Storming**-is that segment where groups determine who is in charge and where you will see the vast majority of arguments and disagreements. This is a very critical stage in team development as this stage sets the tone for how the team performs moving forward. Often teams never emerge from this stage and will continue to fight amongst themselves. The leader should play a fairly active role here in terms of making sure the team members are behaving properly. You may have to intervene in some cases to provide guidance to team members who just don't get along. This is also the stage where your team's true personalities come through. As you build the team, understand that a diverse team will usually perform the best. If you have all Alpha (strong, opinionated, take charge) personalities, there will be a tremendous amount of conflict. Likewise, if you have all Beta (meek, insecure, indecisive), very little will get done. It is best to have a mix of personalities that complement each other.
- **Norming**-this is where the team begins to become cohesive. The infighting has stopped for the most part (there will ALWAYS be disputes, so prepare for that). The team is beginning to create a unified presence.
- **Performing**-this is the stage where the team is performing well together. They anticipate each other's needs, they help and support each other, and each member has found their place within the team. This is the ultimate stage for any team.
- **Mourning**-this is the stage where the team disbands or begins to break apart. Often, team members move on and are promoted to lead their own teams. While this may sound depressing, it is often met with joy and laughter as the team knew that what they accomplished was exceptional and the bonds they built are timeless.

So, what happens if your team doesn't perform? Well, that's a tough call. You have to allow some time for teams to coalesce and bond and learn to trust each other. Depending on the team, this could take months or even years. The key is continuing to provide guidance and reminding the team of the mission. Often though we don't have years for teams to begin to excel. The other option is that you may have a dysfunctional team that may never bond. In this case you need to look at the team members and decide if they are the right fit for the team. Beware of influencers on the team who may be undercutting your authority. I once had a team member who I promoted to a team lead role where his responsibility was to help get new team members up to speed. I placed a lot of trust in this person only to find out that they were destabilizing the team by spreading innuendo and rumors about other team members that were untrue. They questioned decisions behind the scenes while being quite agreeable in front of me. This kind of dissension will quickly kill a team. You need to ensure that the entire team is on board and the way to do this is to be very diligent in terms of the team's overall health and communicate consistently with the team and the individual members.

Chapter 10-Leading Change

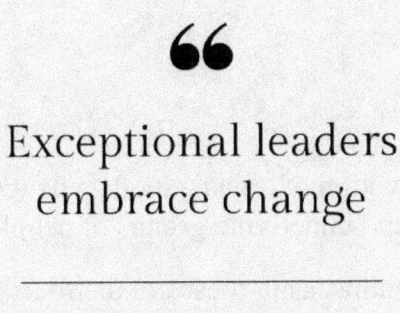

> **"**
> Exceptional leaders embrace change
>
> ROBERT WOHLFARTH

One thing is constant, change is inevitable in every organization. Those that do not change, fail. It's really that simple. As a leader, you are often the one who has to implement the change. Other times, due to market dynamics, change is thrust upon you.

Change is hard for most people and organizations. It is often the fear of the unknown that paralyzes people with inaction. Most people are creatures of habit and not knowing what lies on the other side of the changes that are taking place or about to take place makes them nervous and causes reactions that may not be in sync with the direction you wish to go.

We are as humans hardwired to resist change. Generally, our mind doesn't like things to change and the amygdala, that part our brain that focuses on emotions and threats and is the "fight or flight" part of the brain tends to react and create emotional responses. It is at this most basic level that our fear of change is generated. So, as a leader, you are fighting an uphill battle against the very nature of existence. Wow, talk about a hard job! But the good news is, it can be done by following some basic rules of leading change.

Generally, in any situation of organizational change, you will find 4 different responses and underlying groups of people:

- The enthusiastic-these are the folks who readily embrace the change. They were probably lobbying for it, and they are your cheerleaders. You can use these people to help you in your journey of organizational change.
- The ambivalent-these are the people who don't really care. Often, they have been through numerous changes and are a bit calloused to the whole situation. By involving this group throughout, you can often move them into the enthusiastic category.
- The fearful-this group is terrified of change. Maybe they had a bad experience, or they are afraid that these changes may affect their jobs. With this group, communication is essential to allay their fears. Involve them in the process and make sure they know what is happening throughout.
- The angry-this group will be your most troublesome group. They are outwardly angry at the change and are often very vocal about their feelings. With this group, it is critical to communicate with them and work to restore their support. Be aware that this group may be undermining your efforts

behind your back. If you can, work to get them on board. If you cannot, you may be forced to, unfortunately, part ways with them.

As the leader, it is up to you to guide your team through this process. You are there to assuage their concerns and help them through this difficult time. There are a few ways to help you in your journey.

- Help your team understand the need for change. Often people don't really see beyond their desk and don't understand that organizations often need to change to survive. A good example of this was with a daily newspaper publisher. If there were ever an industry that was under pressure to change, it is that one. While senior management understood the need, others who worked in the printing, design, layout areas didn't want to change because that's all they knew. They feared change, and the organization, rather than making sweeping changes, made a lot of little changes and over the course of several years, they let hundreds of people go, but they did it in small waves While it was necessary, it might have been best to create a plan, communicate that to the people and make large changes rather than numerous small ones which resulted in the "death by a thousand cuts" mentality. Organizational trust evaporated and there were miserable people all through the company.
- Overcommunicate- the saying is that nature abhors a vacuum, and the same is true for organizational change. Without consistent communication, rumors and innuendo will fill the gaps. It is important that they hear the message directly from you, preferably in person. If you ever played the game, Chinese Whispers, where a person creates a message and passes it along through several others and by the time it is repeated, it is often very different from the

original message. Organizations are similar. People perceive things differently and they hear what they want and often change the message, either purposely, or accidently. So, take charge and continually provide guidance and feedback to the team.

- Involve the team-Use your enthusiastic team members to help you. They can often make the difference between success and failure.
- Provide continual feedback-Let the team know where things are and how things are going. This should be mixed throughout your team meetings and your individual one on ones.
- Provide goals-without a goal, the team has no idea how they are doing.

Managing a team through massive change will be one of the toughest things you do as a leader. You will find out a lot about your team and yourself.

Chapter 11-Coaching

> **Exceptional leaders are first and foremost, coaches**
>
> ROBERT WOHLFARTH

Coaching is one of the most fundamental aspects of leading a team. It is the foundation that propels your team toward greatness.

But first, we have to identify exactly what coaching is and, just as importantly, what it is not.

Directing employees to something is not coaching. Coaching is working with each individual to create a growth plan specifically designed for them.

I once worked with a sales leader who, when I questioned how he coached his employees, stated that he coaches them in the weekly sales meeting. He stated that he worked on enhancing skills such as closing or asking better discovery questions. He was a bit shocked when I said that wasn't coaching, that was training. Coaching and training are very different. In training, you start with the assumption that everyone is at the same level of knowledge, and everyone needs to work on the same skills. You might have been in one of these kinds of meetings yourself where you keep thinking, "wow, I already know this". It is the same in many classrooms where the teachers have to work from the lowest skill level and often you end up with those who are ahead of the curve, zoning out and not fully participating. Coaching is working with team members, one to one, to create a growth plan specifically tailored for them.

An excellent tool, the GROW model, can help you with your coaching.

The GROW model was popularized in the coaching industry by Sir John Whitmore in his 1992 book *Coaching for Performance: GROWing Human Potential and Purpose*. Whitmore's acronym stands for:

Goals-set realistic, achievable goals. Remember, most people don't like to change and will initially resist. It is important that you work with your team members to identify those areas where they feel they may need to improve.

Reality, or current reality. What is the current reality? Are they doing well in their current role? Are there areas of deficiency? Do they want to look to be promoted? What skills will they need in the future?

Options-this is where the team member should speak up and provide these options. If you, as the leader, force this process, there will be no ownership of the goals and failure is the most likely outcome. Some questions you can ask them might be: What else could you do? What if this or that constraint was removed? Would that change things? What are the advantages and disadvantages of each option? What factors or considerations will you use to weigh the options? What do you need to stop doing in order to achieve this goal? What obstacles stand in your way?

Way forward, or what you will do-again this area belongs to the employee. They have to commit to an action plan. Personal accountability is critical to effective coaching. Some questions here might be: What do you plan to do? When do you plan to it? Who can help you achieve this goal?

The key to coaching is to establish a baseline for each employee and work with them to grow their skills. The desire to grow has to come from the employee themselves though. It has to be intrinsic. If the employee doesn't see the need to grow their skills, then, as a leader, you have a choice. If their performance is satisfactory, then you may leave them alone. But often, we find that those that don't feel the need to enhance their skills, are often those that need it the most.

Let us look at an example:

Judith is customer service representative who handles a lot of dissatisfied clients every day. She has excellent phone skills, she is polite, and she is well spoken, but she may have a difficult time handling very direct customers. She tends to get flustered and doesn't know how to handle these types of clients.

Her GROW plan might be:

Goal-become better at handling difficult clients. Her goal is to improve her Customer Service Quality Index score by 10 points in the next three months.

Reality: She admits she is not good and could use some help.

Obstacles: Lack of knowledge and experience in how to handle this type of client

Way Forward/Will: Judith will practice, and role play with her manager in the weekly one on one. She will also take a class on LinkedIn Learning on how to handle difficult clients. Additionally, she will listen in to other CSR's who are good at handling tough clients.

I would recommend that you create a worksheet for each team member and use this as the basis for your coaching. It might look like something like this:

GROW Coaching Model Worksheet

Goal: What do you want to accomplish? How will you know when it is achieved?

Reality: What is happening now in terms of the goal? How far am I away from the goal?

Obstacles: What is standing in the way – Me? Other people? Lack of skills, knowledge, expertise? Physical environment? Options What options do I have to resolve the issues or obstacles?

Way Forward/Will: Which option will I commit to? Do I have the desire to do this?

Coaching is such a critical part of being a leader and it is often one of the tougher aspects of the role. Not many people like to be told what to do or how to do it, especially if they have been doing a job for an extended period. You will most likely initially encounter resistance.

Successful coaches know this and don't work from the perspective of the company, they work from the perspective of the employee. Some questions you can ask them:

- What are your goals?
- What are your plans to achieve those goals?
- What challenges do you think you will face?
- What is your timeline to achieve them?
- How can I help you achieve your goals?
- What would you change if you could?
- What do you feel are your strengths?
- What areas do you feel might need some improvement?
- Where do you see yourself in 1/3/5 years?
- What are the most important things in your life right now?

There are several different coaching styles and each one works with a different subset of team members.

- Democratic coaching-This method gives the team freedom and accountability, with the coach stepping in only when needed to keep the process going. Great for very tenured, experienced teams.

- Authoritarian/Autocratic coaching-good for inexperienced team members. You tell them what to do, how to do it and when to do it. This is generally a very one-sided coaching style.

- Holistic coaching-this method believes we are more than the sum of all their parts. Poor performance in one area may be caused by another area, perhaps a personal problem so the coach works on all aspects of a person's being.

- Vision coaching-a laissez-faire style where the leader provides guidance for the team member but is rather hands-off in terms of the details.

The style of coaching you use depends on your personality and your team. If you have an inexperienced team, you will probably have to take a more direct, active approach, but if you have a tenured team, you might adopt a more laid-back approach.

The key to successful coaching is consistency. Coaching should be ongoing, and I recommend weekly coaching sessions to ensure progress.

Chapter 12-Diversity/Equity/Inclusion

> **❝**
>
> Exceptional leaders understand diverse teams perform better
>
> ROBERT WOHLFARTH

Diversity, equity and inclusion or DEI are buzzwords moving through most corporations right now. The shame is that it has taken so long to be brought to the forefront. A diverse team brings numerous benefits to the workplace. From increases in innovation to overall improvements in revenue, diverse companies outperform their non-diverse peers by over 50% (Harvard Business Review).

Diversity refers to race, ethnicity, gender, gender identity, sexual orientation, age, and socioeconomic class. It can also refer to differences in physical ability, veteran status, whether or not the employees have kids.

Building a diverse team can be difficult as we all tend to have unconscious or implicit biases, one of which is the affinity bias. The affinity bias refers to when you unconsciously prefer people who share qualities with you. We tend to like people who think like us, dress like us and maybe we share similar backgrounds. The problem, when you build a team of look-alike employees, is that there tends to be little innovation or thought variance. You create a hivemind and you all look at the problem from the same perspective and this approach doesn't provide depth and breadth in terms of solving the problem. Innovation usually comes from having a fresh perspective and that is what diversity brings to the team.

Additionally, building a diverse team can help you better position products and provide insight into other cultures. There are numerous examples of products being introduced into other countries without properly vetting the name or being tone deaf to their cultural norms. A few examples are:

- When Gerber, a Nestle owned purveyor of baby foods first started selling their baby food in Africa, they used the same packaging as in the USA – the one with the cute baby on the label. Later they found out that in Africa, companies routinely put pictures on the label of what is inside the package, since most people cannot read. Let's just say that the sales numbers were not good until they changed the label.
- When Puffs tissues tried to introduce its product, they were quick to learn that "Puff" in German is a colloquial term for a house of ill repute.
- When Pepsi expanded their market to China, they launched with the slogan, "Pepsi brings you back to life." What they didn't realize is that the phrase translated to "Pepsi brings your ancestors back from the grave."

Building a diverse team provides you with a broader view that usually translates into improved performance. Had these teams had a person who was intimately familiar with those cultures, these mistakes might have been avoided.

Equity is the process of ensuring that processes and programs are impartial, fair and provide equal possible outcomes for every individual. Often this shows up as paying women or a minority less to do the same job. Or ensuring that all of your people have an equal chance at promotions. Always strive to make your workplace an equitable one.

Inclusion is the practice of ensuring that people feel a sense of belonging in the workplace. This means that every employee feels comfortable and supported by the organization when it comes to being their authentic selves. To lead inclusively means to involve everyone. Beware of microaggressions in your workplace. These can come in the form of innocent sounding statements or questions about a person's heritage, race, gender, sexual orientation, age, or socioeconomic class.

Microaggressions are different from outright prejudice and racism. Prejudice usually arises from pre—conceived notions about a population segment. These are born from stereotypes that often manifest themselves as microaggressions. Racism is the fundamental belief that a race is inferior in some way.

While you most likely would not tolerate racism as it is quite blatant, you may not even be aware of microaggressions that are happening in the workplace. Often, these seemingly innocent statements are meant as a compliment, but from the perspective of the receiving party, they are an insult.

Some examples of this might be:

- "Wow, you speak really good English" when talking to a person from another country.
- "I would have never known you were gay"
- "Wow, old man, I'm surprised you have the newest iPhone"
- "You're pretty strong for a woman"
- "All lives matter"

"The workplace should resemble the real world. We live in highly diverse, global environment and we should work hard to ensure our workplace mimics the world we live in.

As the leader, you need to create a welcoming environment that is free of this type of harassment. And should you see it, it is up to you to end it.

How do you stop it? Education is critical to ending this type of behavior in the workplace. Often your HR department will provide classes on DEI. It is recommended that you, and your team, participate in them. The problem is that the perpetrators often don't know that these are offensive. They think they are complimenting someone when what they are doing is actually furthering the stereotype. You may have to have one on one discussions with offending team members to help them understand why this type of behavior is inappropriate. Expect them not to fully understand at first though as their implicit biases sometimes blind them.

We discussed one implicit bias but there are several that you need to be cognizant of in the workplace. Unconscious or implicit biases can be centered around age, sex, name, height, and things such as affinity (they are similar to you), halo (they have one outstanding feature), horn (they have a negative feature, i.e., maybe the way they talk), and conformity (they may not think like the others on the team-this is often a great trait, by the way!).

As the leader of the team, it is incumbent on you to ensure that your team feels comfortable and safe and that your team knows that this type of behavior is not tolerated. While there can certainly be disagreement and intense discussion over projects or work-related items, this can never be allowed to become personal attacks.

Chapter 13-Taking Disciplinary Action

> **Exceptional leaders hold their teams accountable**
>
> ROBERT WOHLFARTH

Being a leader means holding your team accountable to their goals and sometimes the results fall short due to a team member's actions or inactions. At some point in your leadership journey, you will have to take disciplinary action against one of your team members.

Disciplinary action should never be punitive and should be designed to alter or change behavioral patterns of the employee. It should be used to guide the employee back toward being a productive, contributing team member. Unless it is an egregious offense, be empathetic, because the goal is to guide the employee to get back on track.

You will run across difficult to manage employees in your career as a leader. Some will be incredibly hard to manage, but a few tips are:

- Document the problematic behavior.
- Critique the employee's behavior, not the employee.
- Be very clear and direct in explaining why the employee's behavior is inappropriate.
- Be consistent. Don't play favorites
- Don't allow that employee to "poison the well"
- Listen to and consider the employee's feedback.

A key point is to never discipline an employee if you are angry. Let's say they just made a massive mistake that cost the company a lot of money. Our first inclination is to bring the employee in and "rip them a new one". Your best bet is to wait a little while until you have calmed down and can speak without emotion. Introducing emotion into the conversation tends to be counterproductive and can degenerate quickly. It is often best to send the employee home and wait for the next day, if possible.

Most companies use a progressive disciplinary method where there are definitive steps that are taken depending on the severity of the offense.

You should always involve your HR department in the event of the need to take disciplinary action. There are very stringent laws and there is always the threat of a wrongful termination lawsuit, and their job is to guide the process to minimize the risks.

The progressive disciplinary action plan usually involves the following:

Verbal Warning-this is just as it sounds. You bring the person into your office or have a one-on-one conversation (remember, we never discipline in public, unless it is absolutely necessary). You let them know what the offense was and then let them know the behavior is inappropriate or intolerable and also let them know that the next step would be a formal warning.

Written Warning-like the verbal warning, this interaction is designed to let the employee know that their behavior needs to change. Usually, this document will require both people to sign and some companies require a third party to monitor the discussion to eliminate any risk.

Final Written Warning-this is often the last step before termination. If the employee has not gotten the message by now, it is often a foregone conclusion.

Suspension-Often companies will suspend an employee for a pre-determined length of time prior to dismissal.

Termination-this is the final and most difficult type of action for both parties. It is highly recommended that there be a third party involved in every termination discussion. Often, employees will become hostile and quite emotional.

Companies also often have offenses for which they have "zero tolerance". This means there is no progressive discipline These might include:

- Sexual harassment
- Willful destruction of property
- Racism
- Violation of security regulations
- Workplace violence

Please check with your company to review their policies on "zero tolerance" offenses.

Terminating a person's employment is a rather draconian measure but one that is sometimes necessary. You should treat this very seriously and reflect on what happened to get to this point.

Some questions you may ask yourself:

- How did it get to this point?
- Was that person the right fit?
- What could I have done to alter the outcome?
- Was there anything I missed?

Terminating a person's employment can have devastating consequences for them and it really should be the last resort. If you thought highly enough of this person to hire them, then do everything possible to keep them.

A bit of advice is to document everything throughout the process. It is also recommended to create file notes documenting every conversation you have with your employees. You can track their goals and coaching plans, their attendance, their work habits, and any potential disciplinary issues that may be arising. You can often spot issues and head them off prior to having to go through a formal disciplinary process.

Terminating an employee is the toughest job for a leader, but should you have to terminate a person's employment, there are some rules to follow:

Principles to Remember

Do:

- Take the employee aside into a private area.
- Be concise, do not drag out the reason for the meeting. For example, you may say, "Sally, the reason I brought you in today is to let you know that we have decided to let you go as of

today". Do not engage in general conversation-get to the point quickly.
- Enlist HR to help and preferably have them in the room or on the phone. This will help prevent legal issues from arising.
- Show compassion for your fired employee — if you genuinely believe he/she has talents that could be useful elsewhere, offer to serve as a reference or provide other help
- This is not a negotiation-the decision has been made. Often employees may try to stall the process and promise to make changes. But taking control of the conversation and being firm but empathetic, will help.
- Communicate the news to your team in person but do not divulge the details behind the decision
- Do protect yourself-an employee who has been fired may resort to violence or threats.

Don't:

- Put off terminating a poorly performing worker
- Allow the terminated employee to take control of the conversation
- Forget to inform your team

The key point is that unless this termination is the result of a business downturn or a corporate reduction in force, the employee should not be surprised. If you have worked with them on a performance improvement plan and you have been upfront with them as to where they stand, then they should understand why. It will not make it easier for either of you but ensuring you have done everything possible to salvage the employee, will help.

But, prior to initiating any form of disciplinary action, please consult your legal and HR teams.

Chapter 14-Handling Dysfunctional Teams

> **Exceptional leaders know that trust is the foundation of an exceptional team**
>
> ROBERT WOHLFARTH

Your role as a leader is to get the most out of your team but building a cohesive team that excels is tough. There are several elements that need to come together to create an exceptional team.

Patrick Lencioni, a renowned author on team building, in his book, *5 Dysfunctions of a Team,* outlines the foundations of what it takes to create a high performing team.

http://acumen.sg/

Issue 1: Lack of Trust-the very core of high performing teams is trust. This may be trust in the company, trust in the product or service, trust in management, and trust in each other.

Without trust, nothing else will happen. Companies have long known that trust is the foundation of exceptional performance, but not a whole lot of companies have figured out how to instill organizational trust.

Some companies have resorted to trust building exercises like catching a falling teammate, but then they micromanage their employees because they don't trust them.

Trust is hard to acquire and very easy to lose. It only takes one event to lose the trust of the team. This is where your core foundational values play a key role. The key to building trust and maintaining trust is communication. There will always be situations where the company has to make a decision that might disrupt the team's trust, but open and honest communication will help to preserve the trust.

As a leader there will come a time when you are faced with a difficult challenge. Maybe the company has changed their return policy, or a new product has multiple issues, or customer service is not performing well, and it is causing problems in your department. Or maybe the company has to downsize, and a number of people are about to lose their jobs. These situations can and will arise and as the leader, you are expected to continue to uphold the performance of your department while minimizing the impact of the disruption. During these periods' communication is critical, both group and one to one to allay fears.

The number one cause of dysfunctional teams is the lack of trust. If the members do not trust each other, they will devolve into fiefdoms where you have groups battling each other. The answer to this is to ensure that the team is focused on the mission and to ensure that you are concentrating on rewarding the right behaviors. Steven Covey, in his book, *The Speed of Trust,* conveys that there are character and competence-based behaviors. Character based behaviors include straight talk, transparency, righting wrongs, respect, and loyalty. Competence based behaviors include getting results, striving for consistent improvement, confronting reality, and clarifying expectations.

You often see issues where multiple departments converge and the handoff may not be smooth, or problems arise after delivery. For instance, Valerie sold a software program to a large educational institution and was told by engineering that the product would work seamlessly with their existing accounting software. Upon installation, that was not the case. The customer was upset, Valerie was upset, the customer care team felt they were handed a problem that was not theirs and they were expected to fix it. Engineering stated they tested it and it worked. Finance is upset because the customer is refusing to pay. Now you have multiple departments angry with each other and pointing fingers.

This situation could quickly escalate and cause irreparable harm as the departments all want to blame each other.

As a leader, it is up to you to ensure this doesn't happen. But how?

You may want to create a storm team or task force with members from the various departments to go through the problem and identify potential solutions. This will require extending trust to each of the team members and providing them with the mission to solve the problem. Ensure that they have a clear understanding of the desired outcome, i.e., creating a happy client, and that the expectation is that they are respectful and focused on finding the solution, not pointing fingers. Often you will find that the team will quickly move from conflict to bonding over this problem due to the fact that they now have a mission to accomplish.

Issue 2-Fear of Conflict. Conflict will arise with any team and any relationship. It is just a fact of life. But teams that trust each other, deal with conflict differently. They are unafraid of sharing their opinion, knowing that there is inherent trust. Dysfunctional teams often fear conflict or use it divisively. Conflict in any team is healthy if it is approached correctly. As the team leader, it is up to you to establish those boundaries.

As you can see in the chart below, there are generally four approaches to conflict. People will react to conflict based on their personality and how strongly they feel their opinion is valued within the team. It is often a "fight or flight" response.

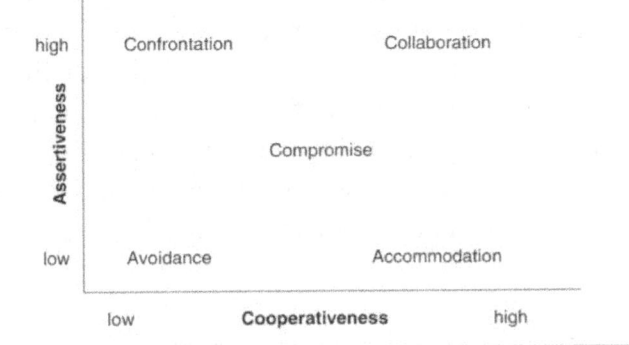

Figure 7.1   Conflict Resolution Approaches

SOURCE: Thomas, K. (1976). In *The Handbook of Industrial and Organizational Psychology* (Marvin D. Dunnette, Ed.). Published by Rand McNally College Publishing Company, Chicago. Copyright © 1976 Marvin Dunnette.

But a few tips are:

- Communicate-teams need to know what behavior is acceptable and what is not. Conflict becomes dangerous when it gets to the emotional stage and then becomes personal. Personal attacks should never be tolerated. The leader should provide guidance on how the team communicates during a conflict. Often conflict arises from perceived slights or personality differences. Some people have a brusque direct communication style that may clash with someone who has a more indirect style of communication. At this point, the leader should mediate between the parties and help them understand their communication differences.
- Focus on the issue-often conflict will arise and the parties will tend to put personal differences ahead of the issue at hand. By focusing on the issue, you can cut through the chatter and keep the team focused. Try to separate the people from the problem-remove the personalization and internalization and have the parties focus on solutions.

- Be aware of personality differences-strong aggressive people will try to dominate the conversation and sway others over to their side. Passive people who may have a better solution often become quiet and sometimes resigned in the face of assertive people, so as the leader of the team, you need to be cognizant of this type of behavior. When you see one of your team members become withdrawn, you can pull them aside and ask why.

Issue 3-Lack of Commitment Teams, in order to be successful, have to be committed to the success of the team. A selfish team member can wreak havoc on generating the desired results.

The team needs to be able to put personal differences aside and focus on accomplishing whatever goals have been set out for them. Employee disengagement comes from a number of sources: lack of leadership, lack of confidence in the company, lack of trust, overwork, and the feeling that their work is unimportant. To ensure a sustained commitment from all team members, you can use these tips:

- Be transparent
- Provide feedback on attainment of goals
- Celebrate wins
- Promote team identity
- Allow for failure
- Clarify roles
- Ask for commitment

Issue 4-Avoidance of accountability. This is a function of lack of commitment where team members lack accountability to the team and to each other. This often manifests itself in one or two team members who slack off. As the leader, it is up to you to rectify this situation quickly. You can do this by:

- Having the difficult conversation-High performing teams are almost self-policing. Team members hold each other accountable and when a member fails to deliver, the team often will produce enough internal pressure to gain compliance to the team standards. But what happens when one team member continually lets the team down? This is where the leader of the team needs to have a conversation to find out why. Is it a *"skill or a will"* issue? If it is skill, then provide whatever training is necessary. If it is a will issue, then further questioning may be needed to find out why. Especially if this was a productive person in the past. If it is simply the wrong fit, then it may be best to move the person off of the team. The key is to do it quickly. Nothing demotivates a team faster than the leader tolerating sub-par performance.
- Communication of the standard-your team should have a standard for how things get accomplished. This is where your mission statement plays a key role. How do you want your team to accomplish its goals and what constitutes success in each role?
- Enforcing those standards-Holding teams accountable to perform against the standards you set is important. What is even more critical is having the team have a say so in creating the standards.

Issue 5-Inattention to detail-often teams become complacent and inattention to detail sometimes creeps in. This may be due to boredom or a lack of interest in their roles. One way to handle this may be to cross train team members to help them stay excited and keep their interest. This serves a secondary purpose of providing insight to team members on other roles and responsibilities. One of the most important aspects of leading a team is to continue to make what may be somewhat boring or dull work interesting. Creating games or contests may help. Also providing an opportunity for interaction outside of the work environment helps to build a stronger team.

Effective leaders are always looking for signs that the team may be experiencing some dysfunction. They not only listen with their ears, but also their eyes. Reading your teams body language will tell you more than their words.

Chapter 15-Managing Virtual Teams

> **Exceptional leaders implicitly trust their remote team members**
>
> ROBERT WOHLFARTH

While some positions have always been remote, 2020 accelerated this for virtually every position. While it has proven to be feasible, it has not come about without challenges.

Working poses a hurdle for both the employee and the leader. Now your meetings take place through a webcam and there is often a loss of unity between the leader and their team.

A few helpful tips when managing virtual teams are:

- Look out for warning signs from your employees. Now instead of having a distinct place to concentrate on their work, your employees are now working from their kitchen tables and living rooms while trying to take care of their kids. Without the benefit of being able to see them personally, you might miss some of the signs that accompany the stress they are feeling. Take time to really connect with your team one on one. Send them little care packages to help them through the day

- Zoom fatigue is a reality. Being on call after call is exhausting especially when you consider the planning that goes into preparing for these meetings. Be mindful of your employee's time and consider just going old school and picking up the phone instead.

- Virtual employees often feel like they are on an island and really don't have the camaraderie that others have in the office. Consider teaming up your virtual team members and having them connect weekly to help them stay linked to the team.

- Respect your teams time zones-having team all over the country or all over the world makes leading them a challenge. Especially if you want to hold a team meeting. Please be respectful of their personal time.

- Beware of the "always on" mentality-being virtual has its benefits but one of the biggest drawbacks is the notion being too available. With programs like Slack in place, it is hard to escape work. People need time to rest and disconnect and recharge. Don't expect your teams to be responsive at all hours of the day and night unless it is absolutely necessary.

- Stay secure-accessing work systems from off premise can compromise system security. You do not have on-site protection from malware and viruses and bad actors can quickly gain access to your company's most sensitive information. Please work with your IT department to ensure that your team members have the proper equipment and security measures in place. Something as simple as working from a hotspot in a coffee shop can cause problems.

Leading virtual teams means being more cognizant of your team's rhythm and listening beyond the words they say. For instance, if one of your more positive team members begins to sound a little more negative than usual, probe and find out what's going on. And use the phrase, "how can I help?" often with your team.

Chapter 16-Recognition

> Exceptional leaders understand recognition is a powerful motivator
>
> Robert Wohlfartth

Have you ever walked into an office and seen the employee of the month plaques on the wall that stopped in 2005? These are sad little reminders of the fact that formal recognition programs often start with great intent, but usually fall by the wayside.

Exceptional leaders understand the power of recognition and use it wisely. Appreciating the hard work your team members put in and recognizing them for these efforts will go a long way toward creating an outstanding team.

Effective employee recognition is often cited as the factor that determines true employee satisfaction.

We surveyed thousands of employees asking the question "What is the one thing your manager can do for you?"

The results are stunning and an affirmation that recognition is critical to a leader's success.

Employees crave recognition and should be rewarded for outstanding contributions. But there are a few things you should keep in mind when it comes to recognizing employees.

-**Be relevant**- according to a 2021 study by O.C. Tanner, a renowned recognition and rewards company, 87% of employees felt their company's employee recognition program was stale or outdated. The best recognition is often the simplest. Just say thank you to your employees for what they do. But be genuine.

-**Be consistent**- If you have ever raised a child, you know how important consistency is. Telling a child one time not to do something generally doesn't work. Conversely, telling them only once not to give up when they encounter a tough problem doesn't work either. Children need continual reinforcement on both sides to reach their potential. The same is true for employees and team members. Consistent feedback and recognition are critical for them to reach their peak.

-**Be timely**- Dog trainers will tell you that if you do not catch Fido in the act of chewing your shoe, then it is best not to discipline him/her at all, because they will not associate the punishment with the act. This also applies to team members. Recognizing an act that occurred last year or last quarter or even last month loses its effectiveness. Recognition works best when it is delivered at the time of the behavior that is to be rewarded.

-**Be inclusive**-Often when you see those sad little employees of the month plaques, you see the same name over and over. While that person might be an exemplary employee, the reality is that there were other employees who might have been deserving of the award. Often this type of exclusionary program leads to a broken culture. Instead of recognizing one person, recognize teams or departments. This will build continuity and trust among the team members.

There are three different types of recognition in companies:

   -Formal company wide recognition programs-While these programs can certainly drive employee behaviors, I have found that, quite often, they are not all inclusive. Often these programs revolve around the sales teams and neglect to include everyone in the company who contribute to the success of the sales team. So, while the top sales winners are jetting off to President's Club in some fabulous location, the sales support team who books the orders, the marketing team who markets the products and generates the leads, the engineers who actually build the product and many others are sitting back in their offices.

Instituting a sales incentive program is great, but the company should also create other recognition programs to praise and appreciate those other people who are equally as important to the overall success of the company.

Having a great formal recognition program in place will help with employee engagement, retention, and recruitment.

   -Peer to peer recognition- Some of the best companies employ peer to peer recognition programs as these tend to recognize behavior that may not be visible to the leader. Imagine that a salesperson lands a very large account and gets the recognition and the plaudits for landing this account. Behind the scenes though this was a joint effort among many departments such as finance, product development, sales support, legal, and many others. Peer to peer recognition tends to build tighter teams and helps to acknowledge those team members whose contributions are essential but not always visible.

Leader to team member- As the leader of your team, the most effective form of recognition is the simplest. Just tell them thank you for a job well done. And do it frequently. Giving them small tokens of appreciation also goes a long way. A couple of ideas might be handwritten thank you notes, thank you notes to spouses/partners, gift baskets, custom printed t-shirts, recognition in team meetings, and remembering their birthdays.

Recognition is not an occasional thing; it is an everyday thing. The very best companies know that engaged employees are happy employees and happy employees make for happy customers. Engaged employees consistently perform better and take less sick time.

So, make it a habit to thank your team members for what they do and create an atmosphere where peers recognize each other's contribution.

Chapter 17-Politics, Performance, and Perception

> **❝**
>
> Exceptional leaders understand the three P's-Politics, Performance and Perception

ROBERT WOHLFARTH

In the boxing ring, you hear the term, protect yourself at all times. This is also true for leaders. While you may be transparent, honest, and upfront, not all of your cohorts are. Whether it is because they are ultra-competitive or they view you as a threat to their rise in the organization, backstabbing is unfortunately a real thing in the business world.

Early in my career, one of my mentors gave me a speech about the 3 P's: Politics, Performance and Perception. He stated that these three words determined your success in an organization. Performance is the easiest as that is the one over which you have the most control. You can better manage performance because you have direct control over it most of the time. Often there are things out of your control or that rely on others doing their job and this leads to P number two-Perception. This is how you are perceived in the organization. Do people trust you and want to help you or do they view you as something else? Do you keep your promises?

Perception is critically important. There is a saying that *"all of the important decisions about you will be made when you are not in the room"* and it is true. Perception may also be known as "executive presence" or gravitas. A few tips to help you develop a strong executive presence are:

Articulate your vision- One of the most important parts of inspiring confidence is having a compelling vision as we discussed in an earlier chapter. It should be a well-conceived notion of what you and your team are working to accomplish. You should be able to communicate your vision clearly in any circumstance, whether a short elevator ride with a senior executive, a meeting with your team or a dinner with important stakeholders. A well-articulated, robust vision is ultimately how you make your mark -- it sets you apart, and it's a powerful tool for inspiring confidence.

Be cognizant of how others experience you. People with a strong executive presence have a very keen understanding of how they're perceived by others. They have a strong Emotional Quotient in that they understand and manage their emotions and how they respond in times of stress well. That is essential as you climb to more senior levels and your span of control expands, you become increasingly reliant on others for your effectiveness. This means they need to trust you and your judgement.

Develop your communication skills. Exceptional leadership is ultimately about communication, and people with great executive presence are excellent communicators in all facets-verbal, written and in-person or virtually. Your body language is an incredibly important factor to consider when communicating. You may want to record yourself and you may be surprised at what you see and hear. Your body language communicates over 80% of your message.

Become an active listener- active listeners focus on the person and not on crafting a response. They listen with all of their senses to get a better read on what is being said.

Cultivate your network- Exceptional leaders understand that companies are composed of complex, interwoven relationships and that there will sometimes be a diversity of opinions and competing agendas. Organizational politics are simply the natural dynamic that arises when people work together. People with strong executive presence are good at cultivating a network of relationships and developing the political savvy to influence challenging situations in a productive direction.

Learn to operate effectively under stress. People with good executive presence present themselves as calm, composed, well-prepared and in control at all times. That inspires the confidence that they're ready to take on even more responsibility. A tool that many people use in high stress situations is square breathing-breathe in for 4 seconds, hold for 4 seconds, breathe out for 4 seconds and hold for 4 seconds. This exercise will calm you and allow you to develop better focus.

Make sure your appearance isn't a distraction. Unfortunately, people do judge you by your appearance. You want to ensure that your first impression inspires confidence. That doesn't mean trying to look like a fashion model. Rather, make sure your appearance is appropriate for the setting and the company culture, and that it is consistent with others at the level you aspire to. Pay attention to your clothing choices, tailoring and grooming, and make sure there's nothing about your appearance that will distract from the impression you want to leave.

Perception and politics are often comingled and act as one. Not to be negative, but not everyone has your best interest at heart and will often do things to hurt your career.

While there may be no way to prevent this from happening, there are steps you can take to protect yourself:

- Be careful what personal information you share with anyone.
- Don't over identify with your group, i.e.," going native" – no friends, no partying with anyone, anywhere in your organization. Maintain a respectable distance. If you hire them, you have to be able to fire them.
- Don't complain downstream– never complain to your team. It makes you seem powerless.
- Don't complain laterally to peers – it accomplishes nothing and enables backstabbers.
- Never ignore customer issues - HANDLE CUSTOMER ISSUES IMMEDIATELY. NOTHING angers a boss more than customer escalations…NOTHING!!!! This will wreck your PERCEPTION faster than anything.
- Don't empathize with staff about why they aren't succeeding. Don't enable them to feel sorry for themselves. Coach them and provide them with the tools to improve but they have to understand their role is to uphold the standards of the role.
- Never make promises to your organization you can't keep – this is an instant morale killer and the sign of a powerless leader.
- Don't hold on to performance problems too long – coach them but if they don't improve and don't care to improve, follow the process, and get rid of them quickly. It won't get better. There is a saying to hire slow but fire fast if you know there are not the right fit.
- Don't be afraid to make a decision –You don't always make the right decision, but any good boss will respect you for making it as opposed to doing nothing.
- Don't be a manager, be a leader – Be in the field, with the organization. The administrative tasks can be done afterhours. If

they know you care and are with them, they will claw through walls for you.
- Do not mix business and pleasure. Getting romantically involved with a team member is often a recipe for disaster. Keep a distance while in social settings with your team.

Managing your three P's is essential to your success in your role as a leader. There are potential pitfalls throughout your journey but keep in mind that mistakes often help you to grow as a leader.

Summary

> **Exceptional leaders lead their teams to accomplish more than the team thought possible**
>
> ROBERT WOHLFARTH

Becoming a leader is an incredible opportunity to positively impact the lives of others. It will often test you in ways you never thought possible, but it is so rewarding.

It is also a position that is often handed to someone with very little guidance on how to succeed. Find yourself a mentor or several mentors and learn from their experience.

The old adage that it is lonely at the top is true. Once you become a leader there needs to be a bit of detachment in how you interface with your team. You have to be able to make hard decisions on behalf of the company and your team members and that is difficult to do when you are too closely involved with team members.

Creating a culture of shared ownership of the departmental goals and creating your personal leadership philosophy will lay the foundation for a successful entree into your leadership journey.

Keep in mind that there is no such thing as a perfect leader. Expect to make mistakes and learn from them. Encourage the same from your team.

Don't let the power of your position go to your head. Stay humble and realize that your purpose is to help your team members to become better employees AND better people.

Don't ask your team to do anything you would not do yourself. Get in the trenches with them and help them succeed.

Always be authentic in your approach. People will test you constantly and your consistent application of high standards will determine your overall success as a leader.

Most of all, please understand that your role as a leader can have a profound effect on people's lives. Never take your position for granted or become jaundiced and uncaring. Just remember the quote we referenced in the beginning that **"people will forget what you said, people will forget what you did, but people will never forget how you made them feel."**

Good luck on your journey!

About the author

Robert Wohlfarth is the CEO of The Nascent Group, a leadership consulting firm which has advised companies all over the world. He has founded several successful companies and has led high performing sales, marketing, customer service and operations teams for over thirty years with several international companies.

www.ingramcontent.com/pod-product-compliance
Lightning Source LLC
Chambersburg PA
CBHW070808220526
45466CB00002B/598